139029
2.5

E CYCLE OF A

Cow

By Colleen Sexton

BLASTOFF!
3
READERS

Note to Librarians, Teachers, and Parents:

Blastoff! Readers are carefully developed by literacy experts and combine standards-based content with developmentally appropriate text.

Level 1 provides the most support through repetition of high-frequency words, light text, predictable sentence patterns, and strong visual support.

Level 2 offers early readers a bit more challenge through varied simple sentences, increased text load, and less repetition of high-frequency words.

Level 3 advances early-fluent readers toward fluency through increased text and concept load, less reliance on visuals, longer sentences, and more literary language.

Level 4 builds reading stamina by providing more text per page, increased use of punctuation, greater variation in sentence patterns, and increasingly challenging vocabulary.

Level 5 encourages children to move from "learning to read" to "reading to learn" by providing even more text, varied writing styles, and less familiar topics.

Whichever book is right for your reader, Blastoff! Readers are the perfect books to build confidence and encourage a love of reading that will last a lifetime!

This edition first published in 2011 by Bellwether Media, Inc.

Library of Congress Cataloging-in-Publication Data
Sexton, Colleen A., 1967–
  The life cycle of a cow / by Colleen Sexton.
    p. cm. – (Blastoff! readers. Life cycles)
  Summary: "Developed by literacy experts for students in grades kindergarten through three, this book follows cows as they transform from birth to adult. Through leveled text and related images, young readers will watch these creatures grow through every stage of life"–Provided by publisher.
  Includes bibliographical references and index.
  ISBN 978-1-60014-451-6 (hardcover : alk. paper)
  1. Cows–Life cycles–Juvenile literature. I. Title.
  SF197.5.S49 2010
  636.2–dc22
                                        2010000706

Printed in the United States of America, North Mankato, MN.
080110   1162

Contents

bull

Cows are large farm animals. The females are known as cows. The males are called **bulls**.

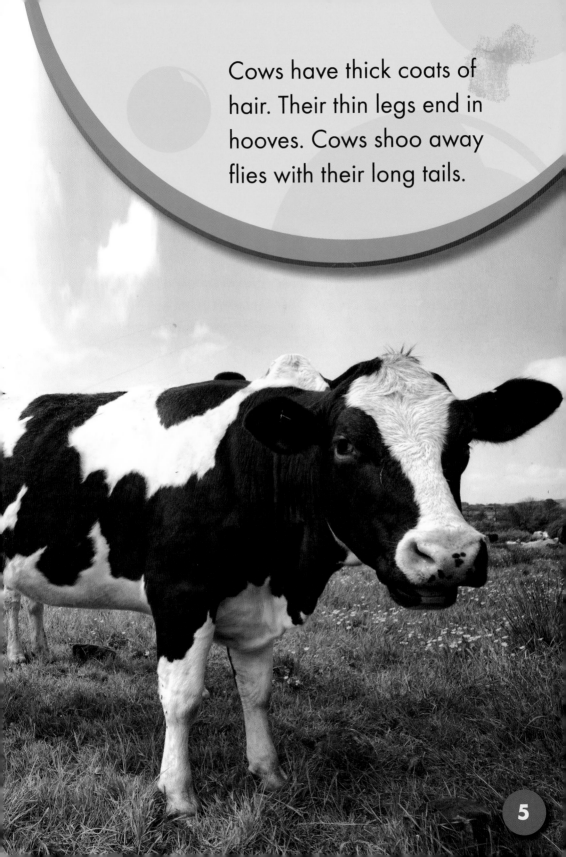

Cows have thick coats of hair. Their thin legs end in hooves. Cows shoo away flies with their long tails.

udder

This cow is a **dairy cow**. She has an **udder** that holds milk. All dairy cows are female.

Cows grow in stages. The stages of a cow's **life cycle** are birth, **calf**, and adult.

birth

calf

adult

A cow gives birth to a calf. The calf is a female. She is wet and weighs 90 pounds (41 kilograms).

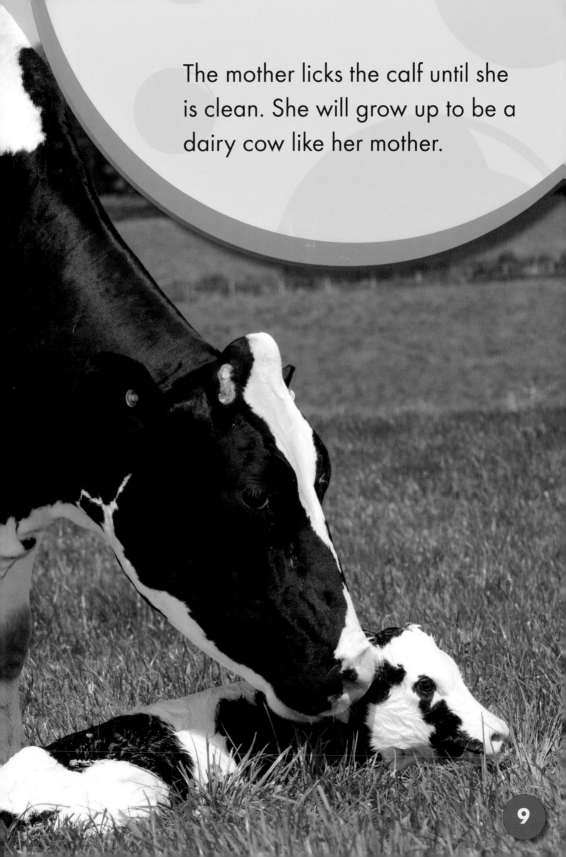

The mother licks the calf until she is clean. She will grow up to be a dairy cow like her mother.

The calf then stands up. She tries to walk on shaky legs. She moves to drink milk from her mother's udder.

The first milk from the mother is special. It will help the calf fight **germs** and stay healthy.

The calf soon leaves her mother to live with other calves.

The calf drinks a mix of dried milk and water. A mix of grains and **vitamins** is added to her diet when she is one week old.

The calf sleeps a lot. Sleeping gives the calf energy. She gets bigger and stronger every day.

The calf is called a **heifer**. Heifers are female calves that have not yet given birth.

The heifer weighs about 400 pounds (181 kilograms) when she is six months old. She eats hay, **silage**, and grain. She drinks a lot of water.

The heifer **grazes** in fields in spring and summer. The heifer grows quickly. She gains nearly 2 pounds (1 kilogram) each day.

The heifer is ready to **mate** with a bull when she is about 15 months old.

A calf grows inside the heifer for nine months. The heifer gives birth. Her calf is the beginning of a new life cycle.

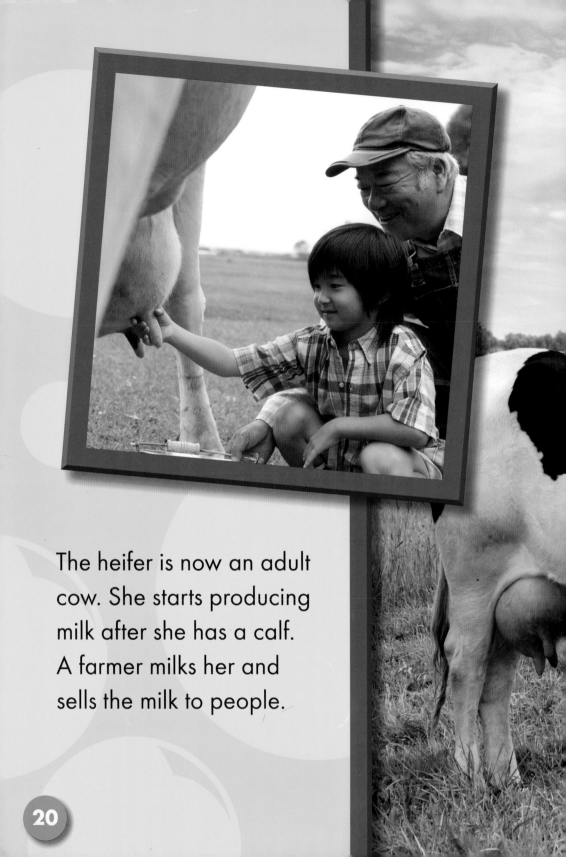

The heifer is now an adult cow. She starts producing milk after she has a calf. A farmer milks her and sells the milk to people.

A full-grown adult cow weighs about 1,300 pounds (590 kilograms) and makes about 90 glasses of milk a day!

Glossary

bulls—adult males in the cattle family; bulls can mate with cows to produce calves.

calf—a young cow

dairy cow—an adult female in the cattle family that has given birth and can produce milk; dairy cows live on dairy farms.

germs—tiny living beings that can make people and animals sick

grazes—feeds on grass; a cow can eat 150 pounds (68 kilograms) of grass a day.

heifer—a young female cow that has not yet given birth; once a heifer gives birth, she is an adult dairy cow.

life cycle—the stages of life of an animal; a life cycle includes being born, growing up, having young, and dying.

mate—to join together to produce young

silage—grass that has been picked and stored to feed cows in the winter

udder—the part of a cow where milk is made and stored; the udder hangs down from a cow's belly; milk comes out of the udder through four teats.

vitamins—substances found in food and nature that help animals grow and stay healthy

To Learn More

AT THE LIBRARY
Green, Emily K. *Cows*. Minneapolis, Minn.: Bellwether Media, 2007.

Mader, Patrick. *Oma Finds a Miracle*. Edina, Minn.: Beaver's Pond Press, 2007.

Ray, Hannah. *Cows*. New York, N.Y.: Crabtree Publishing, 2008.

ON THE WEB
Learning more about life cycles is as easy as 1, 2, 3.

1. Go to www.factsurfer.com.

2. Enter "life cycles" into the search box.

3. Click the "Surf" button and you will see a list of related Web sites.

With factsurfer.com, finding more information is just a click away.

Index